CRIMCOMICS
SOCIAL LEARNING THEORIES

KRISTA S. GEHRING
WRITER

MICHAEL R. BATISTA
ARTIST

CHERYL L. WALLACE
LETTERER

New York   Oxford
OXFORD UNIVERSITY PRESS

DEDICATION

FOREWORD

I always enjoyed reading, but starting at about age nine or so, I became an avid comic book reader, much to the chagrin of my mother, who did not realize that by allowing me to read what interested me, she was encouraging and nurturing a life-long habit of reading. In the summer, I would cut grass, and in the winter, shovel snow to earn some spending money. Then I would ride my bike to all the small stores in the area and spend my hard-earned cash on comic books. I also had some older cousins who had large collections, and whenever I visited them, I would spend hours reading the older copies that were published before my time. And my uncle, who worked at a hospital, would bring me the comics discarded from the children's wards. I vividly remember my friends and I sitting on the front porch swigging "pop" (which is what we call soda in the Midwest), and reading comics for hours on end. Although I read any that I could get my hands on, my favorites were Marvel, especially Spiderman, Thor, and the Fantastic Four, all of which I have enjoyed watching on the big screen. My grown children are always amazed that I know the origins of each character (including the villains), and I suspect that they get a big kick out of

watching me sit wide-eyed in the theater reliving my childhood.

Of course, as I got older, I turned my attention (and money) to other interests, but I always remember the pleasure and joy I got from reading comics. They gave me endless hours of enjoyment and helped transport me to other worlds. I now realize that they were a wonderful vehicle for expanding my imagination and for teaching me about ideas and concepts that I had never thought about before.

When I first learned of Krista's plan to write and translate criminological theories through the wonderful medium of comics, I was excited to see how her ideas would play out in actual form. I was not disappointed. And when I found out that she was going to write a new comic on social learning, a theory that I strongly subscribe to, combining it with one of my favorite youthful past times, I jumped at the chance to write this foreword.

Much of my work over the past several decades has been in the area of correctional rehabilitation, including both studying and assisting programs and jurisdictions in improving the interventions and services offered to justice-involved individuals. I have also conducted numerous workshops and trainings to countless correctional professionals, and at the core of my work and approach is the theory of social learning. I am an avowed behaviorist and I believe that most behavior is learned. I like to tell my students that social learning is a not a theory of criminal behavior, it is a theory of *human* behavior, and it is the processes through which individuals acquire attitudes, behavior, and knowledge from the persons around them. As Krista has written and Michael so skillfully illustrated in this comic, both modeling and instrumental conditioning play a key role in such learning. Unfortunately, as those of us in the crime business know, social learning cuts both ways—we don't always learn just good behavior from others—we also learn bad behavior. And while social learning is a complex process, it is not really a complex concept to understand. After all, despite what we think when we are teenagers, most of us turn into our parents when we get older.

Krista's writing and Michael's illustrations have helped bring the work of Sutherland, Skinner, Burgess, Akers, and Bandura to life, and one can almost imagine being with them as they formulated and tested their ideas. Through the story line, Krista has connected the dots in a way that will undoubtedly help students better understand social learning and the other major theories that comprise the field of criminology.

Let me end by stating that I am honored to write this foreword, and I want to thank Krista for allowing me to relive some of the fondest memories of my youth. I should also add that she was impressed that I still have many of my old comic books, and I had to promise to let her browse my collection the next time she visits Cincinnati.

Krista Gehring and Michael Batista have taken what are often dry and boring subjects and turned them into page-turning and exciting reading. While I am a lot closer to the end of my career than the beginning, I can assure you that if I were starting again today, *CrimComics* would be at the top of my students' reading lists. My only regret is that I did not think of the idea myself.

EDWARD J. LATESSA
University of Cincinnati

PREFACE

Criminal behavior is learned. What a simple and parsimonious way to explain a cause of criminal behavior. And it certainly makes sense, if you consider (or realize) that all behavior is learned. We learn how to read, how to ride a bike, how to behave in social situations—why would criminal behavior be any different?

There are so many things to appreciate about this theory. First, the development of social learning theory in criminology can be traced back to Edwin Sutherland's exposure to ideas that were coming out of the Chicago School of Criminology. He was a contemporary of Robert Park, Ernest Burgess, Clifford Shaw, and Henry McKay and built upon concepts that these theorists were uncovering in their own research. In particular, Shaw and McKay proposed that socially disorganized neighborhoods experienced "cultural transmission of criminal traditions." That is, older delinquents would teach younger generations the tricks and trades of delinquent and criminal behavior. This was apparent when they interviewed delinquents and developed "life-stories" about how they became involved in crime. In 1930, Shaw wrote *The Jack-Roller: A Delinquent's Own Story* followed by *Brothers in Crime* in 1941. These works illustrated cultural transmission, or, put simply, that criminal behavior was learned by youngsters from adolescents or adults.

What a simple, yet impactful, idea. Yet, some scholars were not satisfied with Sutherland's nine propositions. The discipline of psychology was making strides regarding the explanations of human behavior, and by the late 1950s, B. F. Skinner's ideas regarding behaviorism and operant conditioning dominated the field. True to its interdisciplinary quality, criminologists borrowed ideas from psychology to build upon Sutherland's ideas to explain not only that behavior was learned, but also *how* it was learned. Burgess and Akers used ideas from operant conditioning, particularly that of reinforcement, to explain how criminal behavior is learned. When one pulls back a bit to think of not only criminal behavior but all behavior, one begins to wonder whether all behavior is simply shaped by rewards and punishments.

Ronald Akers was not satisfied with this. He continued to develop these ideas by adding the concepts of modeling and imitation from observational learning. These concepts were illustrated in Albert Bandura's Bobo doll experiments, in which adults modeled aggressive behavior with a Bobo doll and children imitated them. Since observational learning is the type of learning most people engage in, its addition really fleshed out the theory.

One of the reasons this theory resonates so much for me is that it was a constant focus in my studies in my doctoral program. Since one of my areas of concentration was correctional rehabilitation, I became very familiar with social learning theory because it is the basis of the most effective programs that reduce recidivism. Since criminal behavior is learned (along with the cognitions that support the behavior), we can put individuals in programs to help them "unlearn" criminal behavior and learn pro-social behavior. These cognitive behavioral programs are grounded in social learning theory and are effective in behavior change. And isn't that what we want to do with offenders? Make sure they don't continue to engage in criminal behavior?

As with any book project, *CrimComics* consumed much time and effort, perhaps more so than a traditional textbook. Thinking about theory—and, in particular, trying to design a work that best conveys the theories in a visual medium—is fun. Still, with busy lives, finding the space in one's day to carefully research, write, illustrate, ink, and letter the pages of this work is a source of some stress. We were fortunate, however, to have had an amazing amount of support during these times from family, friends, and Oxford University Press. We also want to acknowledge the talents of Cheryl Wallace. Cheryl's flair for lettering allowed us to get our ideas across to the readers.

The support of these and so many other individuals has made creating *CrimComics* possible and a rewarding experience for us. We would like to thank the following reviewers: Harold Allen Wells, Tennessee State University; Ellen G. Cohn, Florida International University; Elizabeth Perkins, Morehead State University; Doshie Piper, University of the Incarnate Word; Xavier Guadalupe-Diaz, Framingham State University; Suman Kakar, Florida International University; Elizabeth Bartels, John Jay College; Venezia Michalsen, Montclair State University; and J. Mitchel Miller, University of North Florida. We hope that this and other issues of *CrimComics* will inspire in your students a passion to learn criminological theory.

Social Learning Theories

CHICAGO, 1906.

IN 1906, **EDWIN SUTHERLAND** ARRIVED IN CHICAGO TO ATTEND THE UNIVERSITY OF CHICAGO.

WHILE THERE, HE ENROLLED IN A FEW COURSES AT THE DIVINITY SCHOOL.

HE TOOK A COURSE FROM CHARLES RICHMOND HENDERSON CALLED "SOCIAL TREATMENT AND CRIME."

THE CONCLUSION OF OUR OWN STUDIES IS PRACTICALLY THIS: WE ARE NOT MERELY TO MEDICATE AND DRESS AN EVER OPEN SORE OF PAUPERISM AND INSANITY AND IDIOCY AND CRIME, BUT TO CURE IT.

HENDERSON WAS A MINISTER AND SOCIOLOGIST WHO BLENDED HIS RELIGIOUS COMMITMENTS WITH HIS SCIENTIFIC TRAINING IN SOCIAL PROBLEMS.

SUTHERLAND WAS LIKELY DRAWN TO HENDERSON BECAUSE HIS OWN FATHER WAS A STRICT AND DYNAMIC BAPTIST CLERGYMAN, AND BOTH MEN LIKELY INFLUENCED HIS INTEREST IN SOCIAL REFORM.

SOON AFTER, SUTHERLAND FOCUSED HIS STUDIES ON SOCIOLOGY. HE RECEIVED HIS DOCTORATE IN 1913.

SUTHERLAND TOOK A FEW TEACHING POSITIONS AT OTHER UNIVERSITIES BEFORE RETURNING TO THE UNIVERSITY OF CHICAGO TO BE A RESEARCH PROFESSOR IN 1930. WHILE THERE, SUTHERLAND WAS EXPOSED TO THE IDEAS OF ROBERT PARK AND ERNEST BURGESS,* AS WELL AS THE EMERGING SCHOLARSHIP THAT FOCUSED ON DELINQUENT PEERS AND GANGS.

ERNEST BURGESS

ROBERT PARK

*FOR MORE ON PARK AND BURGESS, CHECK OUT CRIMCOMICS: SOCIAL DISORGANIZATION THEORY!

DO YOU GENTLEMEN HAVE ROOM FOR TWO MORE?

CERTAINLY! TAKE A SEAT!

EDWIN, THESE WERE TWO OF OUR OUTSTANDING STUDENTS, CLIFFORD SHAW AND HENRY MCKAY.*

THEY BOTH NOW WORK AT THE INSTITUTE FOR JUVENILE RESEARCH AND HAVE ACCESS TO SOME REALLY EXCITING DATA!

CLIFFORD SHAW

HENRY MCKAY

OH YES-- I READ YOUR WORK DELINQUENCY AREAS. VERY INTERESTING!

WE ACTUALLY USED YOUR TEXTBOOK IN ONE OF OUR CLASSES, DR. SUTHERLAND. YOUR IDEAS ABOUT THE CAUSES OF CRIME ARE VERY INTERESTING.

SUTHERLAND'S BOOK CRIMINOLOGY (1924) WAS ONE OF THE FIRST AMERICAN TEXTBOOKS ON CRIMINOLOGY.

AH, I'M FINDING THE MORE I LEARN AND READ, THE MORE MY IDEAS CHANGE.

WELL, I, FOR ONE, APPRECIATE HOW YOU CALL FOR A MORE SOCIOLOGICAL FRAMEWORK TO DISCUSS CRIME. MANY OF THE OTHER TEXTS EMPHASIZE BIOLOGICAL CAUSES OF CRIME OR BLAMED INDIVIDUALS FOR THEIR BEHAVIOR.

IT IS QUITE REMARKABLE HOW ONE SOCIOLOGY DEPARTMENT AT THE UNIVERSITY OF CHICAGO INFLUENCED THE THINKING OF SO MANY NOTABLE CRIMINOLOGISTS. THIS SOCIOLOGY DEPARTMENT GENERATED IDEAS AND RESEARCH THAT IS NOW REFERRED TO AS THE **CHICAGO SCHOOL** OF CRIMINOLOGY.

*FOR MORE ON SHAW AND MCKAY, CHECK OUT CRIMCOMICS: SOCIAL DISORGANIZATION THEORY!

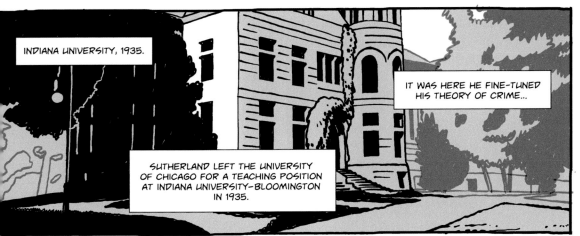

INDIANA UNIVERSITY, 1935.

IT WAS HERE HE FINE-TUNED HIS THEORY OF CRIME...

SUTHERLAND LEFT THE UNIVERSITY OF CHICAGO FOR A TEACHING POSITION AT INDIANA UNIVERSITY-BLOOMINGTON IN 1935.

YOUTH ARE DELINQUENT BECAUSE THEY DIFFERENTIALLY ASSOCIATE WITH DELINQUENTS MORE THAN THEIR LAW-ABIDING PEERS.

FOR EXAMPLE, WHEN I WAS AT CHICAGO, I MET AN INTERESTING CHARACTER NAMED BROADWAY JONES.*

JONES WAS A GRIFTER AND A CON MAN, AND HE WOULD TELL ME THE MOST INTERESTING AND HARROWING STORIES ABOUT HIS CRIMINAL EXPLOITS.

THAT IS WHEN I CAME TO THE CONCLUSION THAT PROFESSIONAL CRIMINALS LEARN THE TECHNIQUES AND ATTITUDES ASSOCIATED WITH THEIR WORK FROM CLOSE RELATIONSHIPS WITH OTHER PROFESSIONAL CRIMINALS.

*SUTHERLAND AND BROADWAY JONES JOINTLY PUBLISHED THE PROFESSIONAL THIEF IN 1937. THE WORK WAS ABOUT JONES'S LIFE AND HOW STEALING BECAME HIS OCCUPATION. IN IT, SUTHERLAND GAVE HIM THE PSEUDONYM "CHIC CONWELL."

MUCH OF SUTHERLAND'S THEORIZING WAS AN ATTEMPT TO ELABORATE ON THE IDEAS FOUND IN THE WRITINGS OF SHAW AND MCKAY AND OTHER CHICAGO SCHOOL SCHOLARS.

HE WAS PARTICULARLY INTERESTED IN AN ASPECT OF SHAW AND MCKAY'S *SOCIAL DISORGANIZATION THEORY* THAT PROPOSED THE IDEA THAT IN CERTAIN NEIGHBORHOODS, VALUES ARE TRANSMITTED FROM ONE GENERATION TO THE NEXT.

SHAW AND MCKAY REFERRED TO THIS PHENOMENON AS *CULTURAL TRANSMISSION*.

GENERATIONS OF DELINQUENTS WOULD PASS ON ANTISOCIAL ATTITUDES AND VALUES TO THE NEXT, THUS PRODUCING AND SUSTAINING "CRIMINAL TRADITIONS" IN THESE NEIGHBORHOODS.

FOR SUTHERLAND, THIS "CULTURAL TRANSMISSION" SIMPLY MEANT THAT CRIMINAL BEHAVIOR WAS *LEARNED* THROUGH SOCIAL INTERACTIONS.

Juvenile Delinquency and Urban Areas

Brothers in Crime

THE GANG

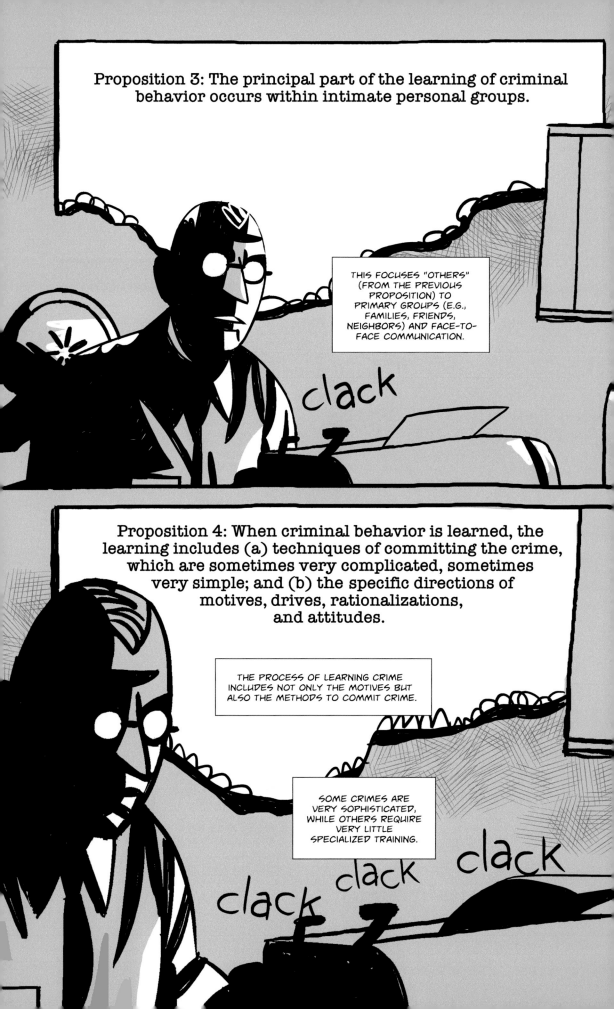

Proposition 9: While criminal behavior is an expression of general needs and values, it is not explained by those general needs and values because noncriminal behavior is an expression of those same needs and values.

ALL FORMS OF BEHAVIOR ARE LEARNED IN THE SAME MANNER. HOWEVER, WHAT SEPARATES CRIMINAL FROM PROSOCIAL BEHAVIOR IS WHICH DEFINITIONS ARE LEARNED, NOT HOW THEY ARE LEARNED.

ULTIMATELY, SUTHERLAND PROPOSED THAT WHAT DISTINGUISHED CRIMINALS FROM LAW-ABIDING PEOPLE WAS THE CONTENT OF WHAT THEY LEARNED. THIS LEARNING DEPENDED ON WHO THEY ASSOCIATED WITH THE MOST. THIS SUGGESTS THAT ANYONE HAS THE POTENTIAL TO BECOME CRIMINAL, AND IT CAN ACCOUNT FOR A VARIETY OF CRIMINAL ACTIVITIES.

BUT SUTHERLAND ALSO CLAIMED THIS THEORY COULD EXPLAIN CRIMES "COMMITTED BY A PERSON OF RESPECTABILITY AND HIGH SOCIAL STATUS IN THE COURSE OF HIS OCCUPATION."

FOR EXAMPLE, IN SUTHERLAND'S WORK *THE PROFESSIONAL THIEF* (1937), HE USES ACCOUNTS OF CONWELL'S LIFE TO ILLUSTRATE HOW DIFFERENTIAL ASSOCIATION WITH THIEVES WAS IMPORTANT IN DETERMINING WHETHER SOMEONE BECAME A SHOPLIFTER, A CON MAN, OR A PICKPOCKET.

HE COINED THE TERM *WHITE-COLLAR CRIME* TO APPLY TO THESE CRIMINAL ACTIVITIES.

THIS CONTACT WAS IMPORTANT BECAUSE IT PROVIDED PROFESSIONAL THIEVES WITH THE TRAINING, BELIEFS, AND COMPANIONS NEEDED TO LEARN AND EXECUTE SOPHISTICATED CRIMINAL BEHAVIOR.

SUTHERLAND INTERVIEWED INDIVIDUALS WHO HELD HIGH POSITIONS IN AMERICAN BUSINESS AND INDUSTRY.

HE FOUND THEY PRACTICED COLLUSION, FRAUD, AND LARCENY AGAINST THE PUBLIC AND FEDERAL GOVERNMENT AND SHARED TRADE SECRETS WITH ONE ANOTHER MUCH LIKE THE PROFESSIONAL THIEVES DID.

THIS ILLUSTRATED THAT CRIME WAS NOT LIMITED TO THE LOWER CLASSES IN THE INNER CITY. FOR BOTH STREET CRIMINALS AND WHITE-COLLAR CRIMINALS, THEIR CRIMINAL CAREERS PROGRESSED FROM NAÏVETÉ THROUGH AN "APPRENTICESHIP" TO ASSOCIATIONS WITH OTHER SKILLED CRIMINALS AS THEY LEARNED TO BE MASTER CRIMINALS.

MEANWHILE, ANOTHER DISCIPLINE WAS ALSO EXPLORING HOW BEHAVIOR WAS LEARNED...

B.F. SKINNER, A PSYCHOLOGIST INTERESTED IN BEHAVIORISM, WAS PUTTING FORTH IDEAS ABOUT HOW BEHAVIORS WERE LEARNED BY STUDYING PIGEONS AND RATS.

DR. SKINNER, HOW IS ALL OF THIS HAPPENING?

HAVE YOU TAUGHT THESE BIRDS TO READ?

YOU THINK THESE BIRDS CAN READ?

HA! WELL, I GUESS THAT IS WHAT APPEARS TO BE HAPPENING!

WHAT WE ARE DOING HERE IS SHAPING BEHAVIOR. WE ARE APPLYING VARIOUS TECHNIQUES TO GET IT TO ACT THE WAY WE WANT IT TO.

FOR EXAMPLE, WE USE *REINFORCEMENT* TO INCREASE BEHAVIOR.

PECK

WE WANT THE BIRD TO PECK THE DISK, SO WHEN IT DOES, WE PROVIDE IT *POSITIVE REINFORCEMENT* IN THE FORM OF FOOD.

THAT IS, SOMETHING PLEASANT HAPPENS AFTER A BEHAVIOR OCCURS.

PECK

WE DON'T DO THIS EVERY TIME, THOUGH. WE INCORPORATE A *SCHEDULE OF REINFORCEMENTS* SO THE SUBJECT DOES NOT KNOW WHEN IT WILL GET THE REWARD, BUT CONTINUES THE BEHAVIOR UNTIL IT DOES SO.

PECK

IF WE WANTED IT TO PECK THE DISK USING *NEGATIVE REINFORCEMENT*, WE MIGHT SEND AN ELECTRICAL CHARGE TO THE FLOOR OF THE CAGE AND KEEP IT ON UNTIL IT PECKS.

BY DOING THIS, IT REMOVES SOMETHING UNPLEASANT WHEN THE SUBJECT ACTS.

WE CAN ALSO STOP BEHAVIOR BY USING *PUNISHMENT*.

POSITIVE PUNISHMENT IS THE APPLICATION OF AN UNPLEASANT STIMULI OR EVENT, WHILE *NEGATIVE PUNISHMENT* IS THE REMOVAL OF SOMETHING DESIRABLE.

BIG BIRD SEE

THESE CONCEPTS OF REINFORCEMENTS AND PUNISHMENTS AND THE WAY THEY SHAPED BEHAVIOR ARE REFERRED TO AS *OPERANT CONDITIONING*.

BIG BIRD SEED

TALKING WITH YOU LATELY HAS MADE ME WANT TO REFOCUS ON THE ETIOLOGY OF CRIMINAL BEHAVIOR AND DEVELOP A GENERAL THEORY OF CRIME.

OH? THAT CERTAINLY WOULD BE A MAJOR CONTRIBUTION TO THE FIELD. AND A SURE-FIRE TICKET TO TENURE!

AND I HAVE A FEELING THAT TICKET IS SUTHERLAND AND OPERANT PSYCHOLOGY.

CLINK

AKERS'S AND BURGESS'S COMMON GOALS LED THEM TO COLLABORATE IN INTEGRATING BEHAVIORIST IDEAS INTO SUTHERLAND'S DIFFERENTIAL ASSOCIATION THEORY.

SUTHERLAND SAID THAT CRIMINAL BEHAVIOR IS LEARNED, BUT WHAT HE DIDN'T ELABORATE ON WAS HOW IT WAS LEARNED.

THIS IS THE MISSING PIECE, MY FRIEND.

Principles of Crimino
CRIMINOLOGY
Behaviorism
Science of Human
Schedules of Reinfor

THIS LED TO BURGESS AND AKERS DEVELOPING *DIFFERENTIAL ASSOCIATION-REINFORCEMENT THEORY* IN 1966.

IN THIS THEORY, THEY RETAINED THE CONCEPTS OF DIFFERENTIAL ASSOCIATION AND DEFINITIONS FROM SUTHERLAND'S THEORY, BUT CONCEPTUALIZED THEM IN MORE BEHAVIORAL TERMS.

PACIFIC Sociological Association

THEY ALSO ADDED CONCEPTS FROM OPERANT CONDITIONING.

SUTHERLAND FOCUSED ON LEARNING THAT OCCURRED WITHIN INTIMATE GROUPS IN WHICH AN INDIVIDUAL WAS TAUGHT BY OTHERS.

HIS THEORY REALLY FOCUSED ON DIRECT INSTRUCTION.

ALL YOU HAVE TO DO IS WAIT UNTIL NO ONE IS LOOKING AND SLIP IT INTO YOUR INSIDE POCKET.

THEN, BURGESS AND AKERS ADDED CONCEPTS THAT EXPLAINED HOW LEARNING OCCURRED USING OPERANT CONDITIONING. THE FINAL PIECE TO COMPLETE LEARNING THEORY WAS THE ADDITION OF *OBSERVATIONAL LEARNING*.

HEY, MISTER? HOW MUCH IS THAT WOODSTOCK POSTER?

IN THE EARLY 1960S, OBSERVATIONAL LEARNING HAD BEEN DOCUMENTED IN *ALBERT BANDURA'S* FAMOUS *BOBO DOLL EXPERIMENT.*

IN THIS EXPERIMENT, CHILDREN WATCHED AS AN ADULT INTERACTED WITH A BOBO DOLL.

THE ADULT HIT THE DOLL WITH A MALLET...

...THREW IT IN THE AIR...

...KICKED IT...

...AND THREW IT DOWN AND BEAT IT.

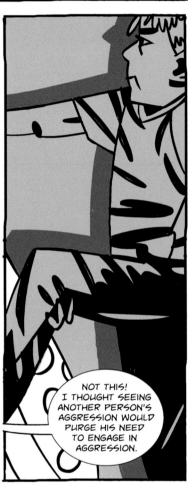

THIS WAS THE FINAL PIECE FOR AKERS'S DEVELOPMENT OF THIS THEORY. MOVING AWAY FROM THE THEORY HE DEVELOPED WITH BURGESS, AKERS ADDED MORE CONCEPTS TO FLESH OUT THE THEORY.

...SO CRIME IS LEARNED BEHAVIOR THROUGH SOCIAL INTERACTIONS WITH OTHERS.

BECAUSE OF THIS, I HAVE CALLED IT *SOCIAL LEARNING THEORY.*

THERE ARE FOUR CENTRAL CONCEPTS TO SOCIAL LEARNING THEORY:

"THE FIRST CONCEPT IS *DIFFERENTIAL ASSOCIATION.* IF YOU RECALL, THIS IS A CONCEPT FROM SUTHERLAND. THIS IS THE PROCESS THROUGH WHICH INDIVIDUALS ARE EXPOSED TO DEFINITIONS FAVORABLE AND UNFAVORABLE TO ILLEGAL OR LAW-ABIDING BEHAVIOR."

GUYS, LOOK WHAT I SWIPED FROM MY BROTHER'S JACKET!

"*DEFINITIONS* ARE A PERSON'S OWN ATTITUDES OR MEANINGS THAT ARE ATTACHED TO A GIVEN BEHAVIOR. THEY ARE RATIONALIZATIONS, ORIENTATIONS, AND OTHER MORAL VIEWPOINTS THAT IDENTIFY THE BEHAVIOR AS RIGHT OR WRONG, GOOD OR BAD. THE MORE A PERSON'S DEFINITIONS APPROVE OF A BEHAVIOR, THE MORE LIKELY IT WILL HAPPEN."

"*IMITATION* REFERS TO THE PERSON ENGAGING IN THE BEHAVIOR AFTER SIMILAR BEHAVIOR IS MODELED BY OTHERS. THE BEHAVIOR DOES NOT HAVE TO BE MODELED BY SOMEONE WE KNOW--WE CAN OBSERVE MODELED BEHAVIOR OF STRANGERS OR ON TELEVISION OR IN MOVIES AND IMITATE THAT AS WELL."

"*DIFFERENTIAL REINFORCEMENT* REFERS TO THE BALANCE OF ANTICIPATED OR ACTUAL REWARDS AND PUNISHMENTS THAT FOLLOW OR ARE THE CONSEQUENCE OF BEHAVIOR. MOST REINFORCEMENTS LEADING TO CRIME ARE SOCIAL (LIKE PRAISE), AND THE PROBABILITY THAT BEHAVIOR WILL BE COMMITTED OR REPEATED IS INCREASED BY REWARDING OUTCOMES OR REACTIONS."

"A CONSIDERABLE AMOUNT OF RESEARCH HAS BEEN DONE TO TEST BOTH DIFFERENTIAL ASSOCIATION THEORY AND SOCIAL LEARNING THEORY. THIS RESEARCH SHOWS THAT CRIMINAL AND OTHER ANALOGOUS BEHAVIORS CAN BE EXPLAINED USING SOCIAL LEARNING THEORY."

"AND RESEARCH CONSISTENTLY SHOWS THAT THE STRONGEST PREDICTOR OF CRIMINAL INVOLVEMENT IS 'NUMBER OF CRIMINAL FRIENDS.'"

AKERS'S CONTRIBUTION TO CRIMINOLOGY HAS ALSO MADE AN IMPORTANT IMPACT IN THE AREA OF **CORRECTIONAL REHABILITATION**.

IN THE CORRECTIONAL REHABILITATION LITERATURE, "ANTISOCIAL ASSOCIATES" AND "ANTISOCIAL ATTITUDES" ARE TWO OF THE **BIG FOUR** RISK FACTORS FOR CRIMINAL BEHAVIOR.*

BOTH CRIMINAL BEHAVIOR AND THE COGNITIONS THAT SUPPORT IT ARE LEARNED FROM ANTISOCIAL ASSOCIATES. RESEARCH SHOWS THAT TARGETING THESE RISK FACTORS WITH PROGRAMS WILL REDUCE THE LIKELIHOOD OF RECIDIVISM.

SOME OF THE MOST EFFECTIVE PROGRAMS FOR REDUCING RECIDIVISM ARE BASED IN SOCIAL LEARNING MODELS. FOR EXAMPLE, *COGNITIVE BEHAVIORAL THERAPY (CBT)* IS AN APPROACH THAT HELPS PEOPLE IDENTIFY AND CHANGE DYSFUNCTIONAL BELIEFS, THOUGHTS, AND PATTERNS OF BEHAVIOR THAT CONTRIBUTE TO THEIR PROBLEM BEHAVIORS.

ANOTHER WAY TO REDUCE RECIDIVISM IS FOR OFFENDERS TO REDUCE THEIR CONTACT WITH CRIMINALS AND INCREASE CONTACT WITH PRO-SOCIAL INDIVIDUALS.

BRIAN, I HEAR YOU ARE DOING REALLY WELL IN GROUP. HOW DO YOU PLAN TO STAY OUT OF TROUBLE WHEN YOU LEAVE HERE?

WELL, I'M GOING TO REMEMBER ALL THE SKILLS I LEARNED IN GROUP, AND I'M NOT GOING TO HANG OUT WITH MY OLD GROUP OF FRIENDS WHEN I GET OUT.

THEY GET ME IN TROUBLE.

BECAUSE WHEN YOU LIE DOWN WITH DOGS, YOU GET UP WITH FLEAS!

24

THIS ISSUE EXPLORED THE DEVELOPMENT OF SOCIAL LEARNING THEORIES. IT BEGAN WITH A DISCUSSION OF EDWIN SUTHERLAND'S DIFFERENTIAL ASSOCIATION THEORY. IN THIS THEORY, SUTHERLAND PUT FORTH NINE PROPOSITIONS THAT OUTLINED THE MAJOR COMPONENTS OF HIS THEORY. HE PROPOSED THAT CRIMINAL BEHAVIOR IS LEARNED IN INTERACTION WITH OTHERS IN INTIMATE PERSONAL GROUPS IN A PROCESS OF COMMUNICATION. THROUGH THESE INTERACTIONS WITH OTHERS, INDIVIDUALS LEARN THE VALUES, ATTITUDES, TECHNIQUES, AND MOTIVES FOR CRIMINAL BEHAVIOR. THE MORE AN INDIVIDUAL LEARNS DEFINITIONS THAT ARE SUPPORTIVE OF CRIME, THE MORE LIKELY HE OR SHE WILL ENGAGE IN CRIMINAL BEHAVIOR. ULTIMATELY, SUTHERLAND PROPOSED THAT WHAT DISTINGUISHED CRIMINALS FROM LAW-ABIDING PEOPLE WAS THE CONTENT OF WHAT THEY LEARNED. THIS LEARNING DEPENDED ON WHO THEY ASSOCIATED WITH THE MOST. HE PROPOSED THAT CRIMINAL CAREERS PROGRESSED SIMILARLY FOR BOTH STREET CRIMINALS AND WHITE-COLLAR CRIMINALS: THEY MOVED FROM NAÏVETÉ THROUGH AN "APPRENTICESHIP" TO ASSOCIATIONS WITH OTHER SKILLED CRIMINALS AS THEY LEARNED TO BE MASTER CRIMINALS. COINCIDENTALLY, SUTHERLAND WAS THE FIRST SCHOLAR TO COIN THE TERM "WHITE-COLLAR CRIME."

ALTHOUGH SUTHERLAND STATED THAT CRIMINAL BEHAVIOR WAS LEARNED, HE MADE NO MENTION IN HIS THEORY ABOUT HOW BEHAVIOR WAS LEARNED. THIS MISSING CONCEPT WAS ADDRESSED BY ROBERT BURGESS AND RONALD AKERS WHEN THEY ADDED BEHAVIORISM (FROM PSYCHOLOGY) TO SUTHERLAND'S THEORY. A MAJOR SCHOLAR WHO DEVELOPED THE FIELD OF BEHAVIORISM WAS B. F. SKINNER. SKINNER PERFORMED EXPERIMENTS IN WHICH HE SHAPED ANIMAL BEHAVIORS USING OPERANT CONDITIONING, WHICH USES REINFORCEMENTS AND PUNISHMENTS TO MODIFY BEHAVIOR. BURGESS AND AKERS INTEGRATED THESE CONCEPTS INTO SUTHERLAND'S THEORY, THUS CREATING DIFFERENTIAL ASSOCIATION-REINFORCEMENT THEORY. THEY REFORMULATED SUTHERLAND'S NINE PROPOSITIONS WITH BEHAVIORAL TERMS AND OPERANT CONDITIONING CONCEPTS.

RONALD AKERS CONTINUED TO DEVELOP THIS THEORY BY INCORPORATING AN ADDITIONAL LEARNING SOURCE: OBSERVATIONAL LEARNING. THE USE OF MODELING BEHAVIOR AND OBSERVING OTHERS IMITATE THE BEHAVIOR WAS SEEN IN ALBERT BANDURA'S BOBO DOLL EXPERIMENTS. IN THESE EXPERIMENTS, ADULTS MODELED AGGRESSIVE BEHAVIOR AGAINST A BOBO DOLL WHILE CHILDREN WATCHED. WHEN THE CHILDREN GAINED ACCESS TO THE BOBO DOLL, THEY IMITATED THE AGGRESSIVE BEHAVIOR THEY HAD SEEN. AKERS SIMPLIFIED HIS SOCIAL LEARNING THEORY INTO FOUR CENTRAL CONCEPTS: (1) DIFFERENTIAL ASSOCIATION, (2) DEFINITIONS, (3) IMITATION, AND (4) DIFFERENTIAL REINFORCEMENT.

PROGRAMS BASED ON SOCIAL LEARNING MODELS ARE SOME OF THE MOST EFFECTIVE PROGRAMS FOR REDUCING RECIDIVISM. THESE PROGRAMS TARGET RISK FACTORS FOR CRIMINAL BEHAVIOR, INCLUDING TWO OF THE BIG FOUR RISK FACTORS: ANTISOCIAL ASSOCIATES AND ANTISOCIAL ATTITUDES. BOTH CRIMINAL BEHAVIOR AND THE COGNITIONS THAT SUPPORT IT ARE LEARNED FROM ANTISOCIAL ASSOCIATES. COGNITIVE BEHAVIORAL THERAPY (CBT) IS AN APPROACH THAT ATTEMPTS TO HELP PEOPLE IDENTIFY AND CHANGE DYSFUNCTIONAL BELIEFS, THOUGHTS, AND PATTERNS OF BEHAVIOR THAT CONTRIBUTE TO THEIR PROBLEM BEHAVIORS. ANOTHER WAY TO REDUCE RECIDIVISM IS FOR OFFENDERS TO REDUCE THEIR CONTACT WITH CRIMINALS AND INCREASE CONTACT WITH PRO-SOCIAL INDIVIDUALS.

Key Terms

Edwin Sutherland
Chicago School
Social Disorganization Theory
Cultural Transmission
Differential Association Theory
White-Collar Crime
B. F. Skinner
Behaviorism
Reinforcement
Positive Reinforcement
Schedule of Reinforcements
Negative Reinforcement
Punishment
Positive Punishment
Negative Punishment
Operant Conditioning

Ronald Akers
Robert Burgess
Differential Association-Reinforcement Theory
Observational Learning
Albert Bandura
Bobo Doll Experiment
Modeling
Imitating
Social Learning Theory
Differential Association
Definitions
Imitation
Differential Reinforcement
Correctional Rehabilitation
Big Four
Cognitive Behavioral Therapy (CBT)

Discussion Questions

1) Provide examples of the following: positive reinforcement, negative reinforcement, positive punishment, and negative punishment. Which of these concepts do you believe is the most effective to use to increase behavior? Why? Which of these concepts do you believe is the most effective to use to decrease behavior? Why?

2) According to Sutherland's theory, what actually causes the criminal behavior? How would this explain both street crime and white-collar crime?

3) Burgess and Akers examined each of Sutherland's nine propositions and revised them with behavioral concepts into seven statements that expressed differential association-reinforcement theory. What are Burgess and Akers's seven statements?

Suggested Readings

Akers, R. (1998). *Social learning and social structure: A general theory of crime and deviance*. Boston: Northeastern University Press.

Akers, R. (2011). The origins of me and social learning theory: Personal and professional reflections. In F. T. Cullen et al. (Eds.), *The origins of American criminology* (pp. 347–368). New Brunswick, NJ: Transaction.

Goff, C., & Geis, G. (2011). Edwin Sutherland: The development of differential association theory. In F. T. Cullen et al. (Eds.), *The origins of American criminology* (pp. 37–62). New Brunswick, NJ: Transaction.

Lilly, J. R., Cullen, F. T., & Ball, R. (2018). *Criminological theory: Context and consequences* (7th ed.). Los Angeles: Sage Publications.

Sutherland, E., Cressey, D., & Luckenbill, D. (1992). *Principles of criminology* (11th ed.). Lanham, MD: AltaMira Press.

Warr, M. (2001). The social origins of crime: Edwin Sutherland and the theory of differential association. In R. Paternoster & R. Bachman (Eds.), *Explaining crime and criminals* (pp. 182–191). New York: Oxford University Press.